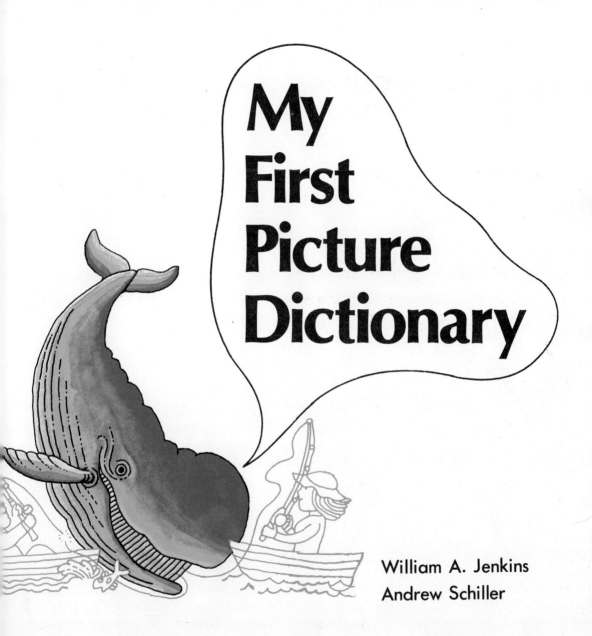

My First Picture Dictionary

William A. Jenkins

Andrew Schiller

SCOTT, FORESMAN AND COMPANY · GLENVIEW, ILLINOIS
Dallas, Tex. · Oakland, N.J. · Palo Alto, Cal. · Tucker, Ga. · Brighton, England

ISBN 0-673-10255-6   ISBN 0-673-10258-0

ABCDEFG
HIJKLMNO
PQRSTUV
WXYZ

abcdefghijk

nnopqrstuv

wxyz

3

Contents

People.   6

Animals.   26

Storybook Characters.   46

What We Do   50

Things   88

Places 146

Words That Help 162

   Some words tell what kind. 163

   Some words tell what color. 168

   Some words help tell
      how much or how many. 169

   Some words tell how. 172

   Some words help tell when. 174

   Some words help tell where. 178

   Some words tell which one. 184

Index. 185

People

artist   artists

An artist paints pictures. Museums have pictures painted by artists.

astronaut   astronauts

An astronaut rides in a spaceship. Astronauts landed on the moon.

aunt   aunts

An aunt is a relative. Penny and Paul have two aunts, Aunt Ruth and Aunt Alice. See the picture for family on page 12.

baby   babies

A baby is a very young child. Little babies can't walk.

People

baker   bakers

A baker makes bread and pies and cookies to sell.

barber   barbers

A barber cuts hair. Barbers work in a barber shop.

boy   boys

A boy grows up to be a man. Boys grow up to be men.

bride   brides

A bride is a woman who is getting married.

bridegroom   bridegrooms

A bridegroom is a man who is getting married.

7

People

brother   brothers

A brother is a relative. Paul is Penny's brother. See the picture for family on page 12.

carpenter   carpenters

A carpenter builds houses out of wood.

checker   checkers

A checker checks the things you buy in a supermarket.

child   children

A child is a young boy or a young girl. Children grow up to be men and women.

People

clerk   clerks

A clerk works in a store. Some clerks sell clothes.

clown   clowns

A clown makes people laugh. Clowns wear funny clothes.

cook   cooks

A cook knows how to cook food. Cooks prepare meals.

cousin   cousins

A cousin is a relative. Penny and Paul have four cousins, Peter, Tim, Jane, and Sue. See the picture for family on page 12.

cowboy   cowboys

A cowboy works on a ranch. Cowboys often ride wild horses.

People

custodian   custodians

A custodian takes care of a building. Most schools have custodians.

dad   dads

Dad is a short name for father.

daughter   daughters

A daughter is a relative. Penny is the daughter of her father and mother. See the picture for family on page 12.

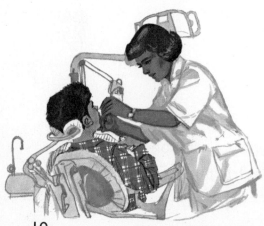

dentist   dentists

A dentist cleans and takes care of a person's teeth.

People

diver   divers

A diver can swim under water.
Divers strap tanks of air on
their backs.

doctor   doctors

A doctor takes care of sick people.

driver   drivers

A driver is a person who makes a
car or truck or bus move.

druggist   druggists

A druggist works in a drugstore.
You buy medicine from a druggist.

electrician   electricians

An electrician fixes lights.

People

family   families

Parents and their children
are a family. All the
people in a family are
relatives.

Grandfather and Grandmother Smith

Uncle Bob Smith

Aunt Alice and Uncle Jim Smith

Cousin Peter Smith

Penny Baker   Paul Baker

People

Grandfather and Grandmother Baker

Aunt Ruth and
Uncle Al Jones

Mother and Father Baker

Cousin Sue Jones   Cousin Jane Jones   Cousin Tim Jones

People

farmer   farmers

A farmer lives in the country and works on a farm.

father   fathers

A father is a relative. Paul's father is one of his parents. See the picture for family on page 12.

firefighter   firefighters

A firefighter puts out fires. Firefighters ride on fire trucks.

fireman   firemen

A fireman is a firefighter.

girl   girls

A girl grows up to be a woman. Girls grow up to be women.

People

grandchild   grandchildren

A grandchild is a relative.
Grandmother and Grandfather
Baker have five grandchildren. See
the picture for family on page 12.

granddaughter   granddaughters

A granddaughter is a relative.
Penny is a granddaughter of
Grandmother and Grandfather
Baker. See the picture for family
on page 12.

grandfather   grandfathers

A grandfather is a relative. Paul
and Penny have two grandfathers.
See the picture for family on
page 12.

grandmother   grandmothers

A grandmother is a relative. Paul
and Penny have two grandmothers.
See the picture for family on
page 12.

People

grandson   grandsons

A grandson is a relative. Paul
is a grandson of Grandmother and
Grandfather Baker. See the
picture for family on page 12.

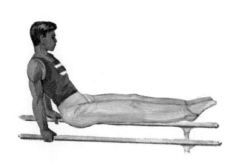

guard   guards

A guard takes care of people or
things. Guards help children
cross the street.

gymnast   gymnasts

A gymnast does many hard exercises.
Gymnasts must be strong.

janitor   janitors

A janitor takes care of a building.
Janitors are custodians.

judge   judges

A judge often has to decide who
is right and who is wrong.

People

librarian   librarians

A librarian works in a library. Librarians help you find good books to read.

lifeguard   lifeguards

A lifeguard works at a beach or a pool. Lifeguards guard people who are in the water.

magician   magicians

A magician can do magic tricks. Magicians are fun to watch.

mail carrier   mail carriers

The mail carrier delivers mail. Mail carriers bring letters from the post office.

mailman   mailmen

A mailman is a mail carrier.

People

mama   mamas

Mama is a short name for mother.

man   men

A boy grows up to be a man. Boys grow up to be men.

mechanic   mechanics

A mechanic fixes engines. Some mechanics work in garages.

miner   miners

A miner usually works underground. Miners dig coal.

mom   moms

Mom is another name for mother.

People

mother   mothers

A mother is a relative. Paul's mother is one of his parents. See the picture for family on page 12.

neighbor   neighbors

A neighbor lives near you. Our neighbors are working in their yard, too.

nephew   nephews

A nephew is a relative. Paul is Uncle Al and Aunt Ruth's nephew. See the picture for family on page 12.

niece   nieces

A niece is a relative. Penny is Uncle Al and Aunt Ruth's niece. See the picture for family on page 12.

People

nurse   nurses

A nurse takes care of sick people.
Some nurses visit homes.

operator   operators

An operator makes something work.
Telephone operators can help you
dial a number.

painter   painters

A painter paints the inside and
outside of houses.

papa   papas

Papa is a short name for father.

parent   parents

A parent is a mother or father. Paul's
parents are his mother and father.
See the picture for family on page 12.

People

people

Men, women, children, and babies are people.

person   persons

A person is any boy, girl, man, or woman. Each one of the people in this picture is a person.

photographer   photographers

A photographer takes pictures. Photographers often work for newspapers.

Pilgrim   Pilgrims

A Pilgrim had to hunt for food. Pilgrims came to live in America long ago.

People

pilot   pilots

A pilot flies an airplane or steers a ship.

plumber   plumbers

A plumber fixes broken water pipes in houses.

police officer   police officers

A police officer protects people. A policeman and a policewoman are police officers.

postman   postmen

A postman is a mail carrier.

principal   principals

A principal is the person in charge of a school. The principal visited our class.

People

relative relatives

A relative is someone who belongs to your family. All the Bakers and Smiths and Joneses are relatives of Penny and Paul. See the picture for family on page 12.

reporter reporters

A reporter looks for news. Reporters find out what is happening and write about it.

salesperson salespersons

A salesperson is someone who sells things.

sister sisters

A sister is a relative. Penny is Paul's sister. See the picture for family on page 12.

son sons

A son is a relative. Paul is the son of his father and mother. See the picture for family on page 12.

People

superintendent   superintendents

The superintendent of schools
is speaking on TV today.

teacher   teachers

A teacher helps people learn.
Teachers work in schools.

twin   twins

Twins are two persons born at the
same time, to the same parents.
Penny and Paul are twins. See the
picture for family on page 12.

typist   typists

A typist operates a typewriter.
Many typists work in a big office.

People

uncle   uncles

An uncle is a relative. Paul has three uncles, Uncle Al, Uncle Bob, and Uncle Jim. See the picture for family on page 12.

waiter   waiters

A waiter is a man who serves food in a restaurant.

waitress   waitresses

A waitress is a woman who serves food in a restaurant.

watchman   watchmen

A watchman guards a building. Most watchmen work at night.

woman   women

A girl grows up to be a woman. Girls grow up to be women.

Animals

alligator   alligators
An alligator lives near water.
Alligators have thick skin.

animal   animals
Dogs and cats, lions and tigers,
are animals. Birds and fish and
insects are animals, too.

ant   ants
An ant is a small insect that lives
in the ground. Ants work hard.

bat   bats
A bat looks like a mouse with
wings. Bats can fly.

bear   bears
A bear is a huge animal that likes
honey. Bears sleep all winter.

Animals

beaver   beavers

A beaver has sharp teeth and a flat tail. Beavers can cut down a tree with their teeth.

bee   bees

A bee is an insect that makes honey and wax. Bees can fly.

beetle   beetles

A beetle is an insect. Beetles have hard covers on their wings.

bird   birds

A bird is an animal that has feathers and wings. Most birds can fly.

blue jay   blue jays

A blue jay is a large blue bird. Blue jays make a loud cry.

Animals

bug   bugs

A bug is an insect. Bugs crawl.

butterfly   butterflies

A butterfly is an insect with
large, brightly colored wings.
Some butterflies only live one day.

calf   calves

A calf is a cow's baby. Calves
run and jump.

camel   camels

A camel can carry a heavy load.
Camels live in the desert. Some
camels have two humps.

canary   canaries

A canary is a small yellow bird
that sings. Many people keep
canaries in cages.

28

Animals

cardinal   cardinals
A cardinal is a bright-red bird.

cat   cats
A cat has soft fur. Cats make good pets.

caterpillar   caterpillars
A caterpillar looks like a fuzzy worm. It turns into a butterfly.

centipede   centipedes
A centipede looks like a worm with many legs.

chicken   chickens
A chicken is a bird raised for food. Chicken is good to eat.

chipmunk   chipmunks
A chipmunk looks like a small squirrel. Chipmunks have stripes.

29

Animals

A colt is a young horse or donkey.
Colts like to run and jump.

cow   cows

A cow is a farm animal. Cows give
milk. Most cows are gentle.

crow   crows

A crow is a large, shiny black
bird with a loud cry.

cub   cubs

A cub is a baby animal. Baby
bears and baby lions are cubs.

deer   deer

A deer is a wild animal. Many
deer have antlers.

Animals

dinosaur   dinosaurs

There is no dinosaur alive today.
Dinosaurs were huge animals that
lived many, many years ago.

dog   dogs

A dog is a good pet.

dolphin   dolphins

A dolphin is a sea animal. It
looks like a large fish. Dolphins
can do tricks.

donkey   donkeys

A donkey is smaller than a horse.
Donkeys can carry heavy loads.

duck   ducks

A duck is a bird that swims and
flies. Some ducks are wild.

Animals

eagle   eagles

An eagle is a large, strong bird.
It builds its nest in a high place.

elephant   elephants

An elephant is a very large animal
with a trunk.

fish   fish

A fish is an animal that lives in
water. Fish have fins instead of
legs or wings. Some fish is good
to eat.

fly   flies

A fly is an insect with wings.
Flies buzz when they fly.

Animals

fox   foxes

A fox looks like a small dog.
Foxes are wild animals.

frog   frogs

A frog has smooth skin and no tail.
Frogs live in or near water.

gerbil   gerbils

A gerbil looks like a small mouse.
Gerbils make good pets.

giraffe   giraffes

A giraffe has a long neck.
Giraffes are tallest of all the
animals.

goat   goats

A goat has horns and a short tail.
Some people drink goat's milk.

Animals

goldfish   goldfish

A goldfish is a small, brightly
colored fish. Goldfish often
live in glass bowls.

goose   geese

A goose is a bird that swims.
Geese are larger than ducks.

guppy   guppies

A guppy is a very small fish.
Some people raise guppies.

hamster   hamsters

A hamster is like a mouse, but it
is larger. Hamsters are sometimes
kept as pets.

hen   hens

A hen is a female chicken. Hens
lay eggs.

Animals

hippopotamus   hippopotamuses

A hippopotamus is a large animal with thick skin. It has short legs and a big head. It likes to swim.

horse   horses

A horse can carry a person or pull a wagon. Some horses do tricks.

hummingbird   hummingbirds

A hummingbird is tiny. Its wings move so fast they hum.

insect   insects

An insect is any small animal with six legs. Flies and bees are insects.

kangaroo   kangaroos

A kangaroo has a thick, strong tail. The female kangaroo carries her baby in a pouch.

Animals

kid   kids

A kid is a baby goat.

kitten   kittens

A kitten is a baby cat.

koala   koalas

A koala looks like a little bear.
Koalas live in trees.

ladybug   ladybugs

A ladybug is small and round.
Ladybugs have black spots.

lamb   lambs

A lamb is a baby sheep.

leopard   leopards

A leopard is a big, wild cat.
Leopards have spots.

Animals

lion   lions
A lion is a large, strong animal.
It has a loud roar.

lizard   lizards
A lizard has short legs and a
long tail.

monkey   monkeys
A monkey is very smart. It is
fun to watch monkeys at the zoo.

mosquito   mosquitoes
A mosquito is an insect that flies.
Mosquitoes bite people.

mouse   mice
A mouse is a small animal with a
long tail. People don't want mice
in their houses.

Animals

opossum   opossums

An opossum carries its babies on
its back. Opossums live in trees.

owl   owls

An owl is a bird with large eyes.
It can see well in the dark.

panda   pandas

A panda looks like a bear. It is
black and white.

parakeet   parakeets

A parakeet is a small bird. Some
parakeets can say words.

parrot   parrots

A parrot is a large bird with
bright-colored feathers. Some
parrots can talk.

Animals

peacock   peacocks

A peacock is a big bird. Its tail feathers spread out like a huge fan.

penguin   penguins

A penguin is a bird that swims but cannot fly. Penguins live near the South Pole.

pig   pigs

A pig is raised for its meat. Bacon and ham come from pigs.

pigeon   pigeons

A pigeon is a bird with short legs. Many pigeons live in the city. People often go to the park and feed pigeons.

Animals

pony   ponies

A pony is a kind of small horse.
Ponies are fun to ride.

porcupine   porcupines

A porcupine is covered with stiff,
sharp quills. The quills keep
other animals away.

puppy   puppies

A puppy is a baby dog. Puppies
like to play.

rabbit   rabbits

A rabbit has soft fur and long
ears. Rabbits are good pets.

raccoon   raccoons

A raccoon looks as if it is
wearing a black mask.

Animals

rat   rats

A rat looks like a mouse, but it is larger.

reindeer   reindeer

A reindeer is a kind of large deer. Reindeer live where it is cold.

rhinoceros   rhinoceroses

A rhinoceros has one or two horns on its nose. It is a wild animal.

robin   robins

A robin is a bird with a red breast. Robins eat worms.

rooster   roosters

A rooster is a male chicken. Roosters crow in the morning.

41

Animals

seal   seals

A seal lives in or near cold water.
Seals in a circus can do tricks.

sheep   sheep

A sheep has a thick coat of wool.
Sheep are raised on ranches and
farms.

skunk   skunks

A skunk is black. It has white
stripes down its back.

snail   snails

A snail is a tiny animal with a
shell but no legs. It always moves
very slowly.

snake   snakes

A snake is long and thin. It has
no legs. It crawls on the ground.

Animals

sparrow   sparrows

A sparrow is a small bird.
Sparrows are brown and gray.

spider   spiders

A spider has eight long legs and
no wings. Spiders spin webs.

squirrel   squirrels

A squirrel has a big bushy tail.
Squirrels live in trees and eat nuts.

starfish   starfish

A starfish is a sea animal that
looks like a star. Starfish are
often found on the beach.

swan   swans

A swan is a large white bird with
a long, thin neck. It lives near
the water and likes to swim.

Animals

tiger   tigers

A tiger looks like a big cat, but it is wild. It has stripes.

toad   toads

A toad looks like a brown frog. Toads often live in gardens or yards. Toads are hard to see.

turkey   turkeys

A turkey is a large bird. Turkeys are raised for food.

turtle   turtles

A turtle has four legs and a hard shell. Many turtles live in or near water.

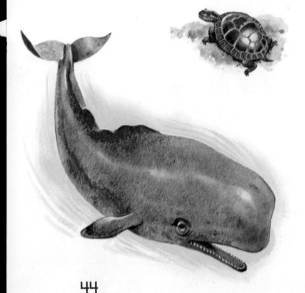

whale   whales

A whale is a sea animal. It looks like a huge fish.

Animals

wolf   wolves

A wolf is a wild animal that looks
like a dog. Wolves howl.

woodpecker   woodpeckers

A woodpecker is a bird with a
strong bill. It can peck holes
in trees.

worm   worms

A worm is a small, thin animal
without legs. It lives in the
ground. Birds and fish eat worms.

zebra   zebras

A zebra is a wild animal. It looks
like a striped horse.

Storybook Characters

A brownie looks like a tiny person.
Brownies help people when no one
is looking.

A dragon is a huge monster.
Dragons breathe fire.

A dwarf looks like a little person.
Dwarfs have magic power.

An elf looks like a tiny person.
Elves are full of tricks.

A fairy looks like a tiny person.
Fairies have magic power.

Storybook Characters

ghost   ghosts

A ghost is a shadowy white figure.

giant   giants

A giant looks like a huge person.
Giants are very strong.

goblin   goblins

A goblin looks like an ugly-looking
little man or animal.

Jack Frost

Jack Frost paints leaves in the
fall. Nobody ever sees him.

king   kings

A king is a man who rules a
country. Kings wear crowns.

Storybook Characters

knight   knights

A knight is a man who does good deeds. Knights wear armor.

ogre   ogres

An ogre is a horrible monster that eats people.

pirate   pirates

A pirate is a bad person who steals ships and buries treasure.

prince   princes

A prince is a king's son. In stories many princes are handsome.

princess   princesses

A princess is a king's daughter. In stories most princesses are beautiful.

Storybook Characters

queen   queens
In stories a queen is a king's wife. Queens wear crowns.

troll   trolls
A troll is a funny-looking creature. Trolls live in caves.

unicorn   unicorns
A unicorn looks like a horse. It has a long horn on its forehead. Unicorns are white.

witch   witches
A witch looks like an old woman. She rides a broom. Witches are mean.

wizard   wizards
A wizard looks like a man. He has magic power. Some wizards are good. Some are bad.

What We Do

answer

Bobby is answering the telephone.
He answered it as soon as it rang.

bake

Dad and Johnny are baking cookies.
They baked a cake, too.

bat

Edith is batting the ball. She
batted it harder last time.

begin

Snow is beginning to fall. It
began all of a sudden. The wind
has begun to blow, too.

What We Do

bend

The strong man is bending an iron bar. He bent one until it broke. He has bent many bars.

bite

George was biting an apple. He bit his finger by mistake. He has bitten two fingers.

blow

Jim is blowing his horn. Pam blew her horn first. All the children have blown their horns.

bounce

The girl is bouncing the ball. She bounced it high.

51

What We Do

break

Bruce was breaking an egg into a pan. It broke on the floor instead. He has broken two eggs so far.

brush

Jane is brushing her hair again. She brushed it this morning.

build

Dave is building a castle. He built a house yesterday. He has built a whole city.

button

Jean is buttoning her coat. She buttoned her sweater first.

What We Do

buy

Mother is buying a car. She bought a red car last year. She has never bought a blue one.

carry

The cat is carrying her kitten home. She carried it across the street.

catch

Jessie is catching the ball. She caught the ball in her mitt. She has caught it every time.

chin

Art is chinning himself. He chinned himself three times without stopping.

What We Do

choose

Sally is choosing a book. She chose two stories. She has chosen a picture book, too.

chop

Louis is chopping wood. He chopped down a big tree.

clap

The girl was clapping. The boy clapped, too.

climb

The cat is climbing the ladder. It climbed a tree yesterday.

What We Do

color

She is coloring with crayons. She colored the flowers yellow.

comb

Tom is combing his hair. Joe combed his hair long ago.

come

The train is coming. It came out of the tunnel and stopped. It has come over the hill slowly.

crawl

The baby is crawling all over the floor. Once he crawled under the table and laughed at us.

What We Do

cry

The puppy is still crying. The puppy cried all night.

cut

Uncle Lee is cutting meat. He cut a big piece of meat for me. He has cut one for you, too.

dance

The girls are dancing at Joy's house. They danced fast.

dial

Barbara is dialing May's number. She dialed the wrong number first.

What We Do

dig

The dog is digging a hole. It dug two holes yesterday. It has dug holes all over the yard.

dive

Sam is diving into the pool. He dived off the board.

do

What is Grandpa doing in the kitchen? He did the cooking. He has done all the work.

draw

Ruth is drawing a picture. She drew a house. Now she has drawn two trees.

What We Do

dress

Carl is dressing for school. He dressed all by himself.

drink

Lois is drinking another glass of milk. She drank milk for breakfast. She had drunk two glasses of milk for lunch.

drive

Mother is driving the car. She drove out of the garage. She has driven to work.

drop

Peg is dropping a letter in the mailbox. She dropped it on the ground first.

What We Do

The baby is dumping his toys. He dumped toys everywhere.

eat

The Martínez family is eating supper. Rosa ate everything on her plate. She could have eaten more.

erase

The teacher is erasing the chalkboard. She erased the poem.

fall

The leaves are falling from the trees. Many leaves fell when the wind blew. Most of the leaves have fallen since yesterday.

What We Do

feed

Carmen is feeding the chickens. She fed them after school. She has fed them twice today.

fight

The kids are fighting. They fought over the ball. They have fought every time they played ball.

find

Danny is finding four-leaf clovers everywhere he looks. He found three in the yard. He has found ten today.

fish

The people are still fishing. They fished all day.

What We Do

fix

Dad is fixing the car. We both fixed my bicycle.

fly

The birds are flying south. They flew out of sight. Every day some more birds have flown away.

fold

Mom and Dad are folding towels. Dad took them out of the dryer.

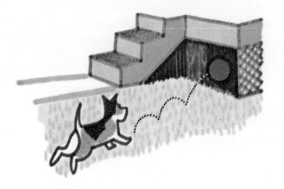

follow

The dog was following the ball. He followed it under the porch.

What We Do

forget

Are you forgetting anything? One girl forgot her mittens. I have forgotten my scarf.

freeze

The pond is freezing. It froze last night. It has frozen a little more every night.

frown

Father is frowning. He frowned when the window broke.

give

Mother is giving me a birthday present. She gave my sister one last month. She has given my brother his present.

What We Do

go

Roger is going to the store again. He went to the store yesterday. He has gone twice today.

grow

The sunflower is growing fast. It grew more last night. It has grown every day.

hammer

The woman is hammering a nail. She hammered three nails.

hang

The monkey is hanging upside down. It hung that way all day. It has hung by its tail for hours.

What We Do

help

Patsy is helping her mother.
She helped paint the wall.

hide

The kitten is hiding behind the
chair. It hid there before. It
has hidden in the closet, too.

hit

Joe is not hitting the ball.
Once he hit it across the street.
Today he has not hit it at all.

hop

The clown is hopping up the stairs.
He hopped down the stairs.

What We Do

hug

She is hugging her dog. She hugged her kitten too hard.

iron

Mother is ironing clothes. She ironed four dresses after work.

jump

Nancy is jumping up and down. She jumped over the flowers.

kick

George was kicking his ball. He kicked it into a tree.

What We Do

know

Do you know that boy? I knew his sister in kindergarten. I have never known his name.

laugh

The boy was laughing at the clown. He laughed very hard.

lie

Jack wanted to lie down. He lay down after lunch. He has lain on the couch for an hour.

make

Sue is making peanut-butter cookies. Moy made ginger cookies. They have made lots of cookies today.

What We Do

milk

The farmer is milking the brown cow. He milked the other cows.

mix

Bobby and Jane are mixing paste. They mixed paste for their teacher.

mop

Herb is mopping the kitchen floor. He mopped all the floors.

move

A new family is moving into our building. The other family moved out last week.

What We Do

oil

Father is oiling the mower.
He oiled it last fall.

open

Sally is opening her book.
She opened it to a picture.

orbit

The spaceship is orbiting the moon.
It orbited the earth first.

paint

Jim is painting the fence white.
Someone painted it blue.

What We Do

paste

Wendy is pasting pictures in the book. She pasted many pictures.

patch

Joe is patching his beach ball. He patched it in two places.

peel

Mom and Dad are peeling apples. They peeled enough for ten pies.

plant

Father is planting trees. He planted two trees in our front yard and two in the back yard.

What We Do

play

Ann is playing the piano. She just played a new song.

point

Henry is pointing at the blue kite. Bill pointed at the red kite.

pour

Frank is pouring milk. He poured a glassful for you.

print

Jim is printing his name again. He printed it too big.

What We Do

pull

The dog was pulling the wagon all day. He pulled it slowly.

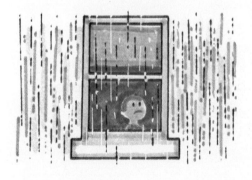

push

Dad is pushing the door shut. He pushed it open.

rain

It is raining hard. It rained all afternoon.

rake

Rita is raking the yard. She raked some leaves into a pile.

What We Do

ride

The dog is riding in the car. It rode to the store. It has ridden many times.

rise

The sun is rising. Dan was up when it rose yesterday. It has risen later every day.

rock

The ship was rocking. It rocked in the waves.

roll

The ball is still rolling. It rolled all the way down the hill.

What We Do

rope

The cowboy is roping another calf.
He roped the first calf quickly.

run

Neil is running up the stairs. He
ran down the street fast. He has
run all the way home.

saw

Two men are sawing a tree down.
They sawed trees yesterday.

say

Mother was saying no. She said it
to George. She has said it to
George quite often.

What We Do

scare

The noise is scaring the baby. It scared the cat, too.

see

Tony is seeing a movie on TV. He saw it last week, too. He has seen many movies on TV.

sew

Bonny and Dale are sewing their tent. They sewed two torn places.

shake

Don't shake too much pepper on your meat. I shook a lot on mine. Don has shaken salt on his potato.

What We Do

shovel
Frank is shoveling snow. He shoveled the driveway.

show
Joanne is showing us her frog. She showed it at school. She has shown it to everyone.

shrink
Carol's dress is shrinking. It shrank a little when it was washed. It has shrunk more in the rain.

shut
Mother is shutting the windows. She shut them because it rained. Have you shut the door?

What We Do

sing

Barbara is singing to the baby.
She sang some quiet songs. She has
sung ten songs.

sink

John's toy boat was sinking. It
sank to the bottom of the pool.
It has sunk fast.

skate

She is skating on the sidewalk.
She skated down a hill.

sleep

The baby is sleeping. He slept
almost all day. He has slept a lot.

What We Do

slide

Fred was sliding on the ice. He slid into a tree. Have you ever slid into a tree?

smile

Lin is smiling for her picture. She smiled at the camera.

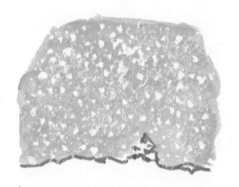

snow

It is snowing again. It snowed all day yesterday.

spade

Paula is spading the garden. She spaded a flower bed yesterday.

What We Do

speak

The principal is speaking again.
She spoke last week. She has
spoken three times.

spill

Henry is spilling the paint. He
spilled some of it on the floor.

splash

Dave's dog is splashing water on
the floor. He splashed a lot of
water on Dave and Julie, too.

spread

Bud is spreading peanut butter on
his bread. He spread a lot on one
slice. He has spread some for you.

What We Do

squeeze

Lois is squeezing orange juice.
She squeezed it into a glass.

stand

The man is standing in the bus. He
stood all the way home. Have you
ever stood all the way downtown?

step

Larry is stepping over a puddle.
He stepped over two puddles.

stick

Winnie Mae is sticking pins in the
cloth. I stuck pins in some cloth,
too. She has stuck her finger!

What We Do

stir

María is stirring the paint. She stirred it to mix it.

stop

Father is stopping the car. He stopped it in the driveway.

sweep

Hank and Heidi are sweeping the garage. They swept the driveway, too. Have they swept the walk yet?

swim

Princess is swimming in the pool. She swam under the diving board. She has swum all around the edge.

What We Do

swing

Karen is swinging in the swing.
She swung high. She has swung
higher than Sue.

take

Wally is taking another doughnut.
He took one for me. We have taken
only two.

talk

John is talking to Ruth. He talked
about school.

tear

Frisky is tearing paper. He tore
the magazine. He has torn every
magazine in the house.

What We Do

tell

Gail was telling a story. She told the story well. She has told many stories to the class.

throw

Jack was throwing the ball. He threw it to Tom. Tom has thrown the ball in the bushes again.

tie

Carol is tying her shoe. She tied her brother's shoe, too. She had tied her brother's tie before.

toast

Jim is toasting marshmallows. He toasted the last one too long.

What We Do

touch

The baby was touching the stuffed bear. He touched it gently.

trim

Kathy and Matt are trimming the bush. They trimmed all the bushes.

turn

Kiku is turning around. She turned around once before.

wade

Bobby is wading in the pool. He waded there yesterday.

What We Do

walk

Ann is walking to school. She walked home yesterday.

wash

We are washing the car. We washed it inside and out.

watch

Andy was watching a movie on TV. First he watched a cartoon.

water

Jill is watering her garden. She watered every flower.

What We Do

wear

Sue is wearing her new coat. She
wore it to the party. She has
worn it twice.

weave

Alice is weaving a basket. She
wove part of it in school. She
has woven two other baskets.

weigh

Mother is weighing the baby again.
She weighed him only yesterday.

whistle

Pete was whistling for the dog.
He whistled as loud as he could.

What We Do

wind

Joe is winding the clock. He wound
it last week. He hasn't wound it
since it stopped.

wink

Father is winking at the baby.
The baby winked at me.

work

Uncle Ben is working in the yard.
He worked all day.

wrap

Lucy is wrapping a present. She
wrapped it in blue paper.

What We Do

write

Pam is writing her name. She wrote it on paper. She has written it carefully this time.

yawn

The dog is yawning. It yawned all morning. It's a lazy dog.

yell

Sue is yelling at David. She yelled at Earl, too. They ran through her castle.

zip

Bert was zipping his jacket. He zipped it to the top.

Things

airplane   airplanes

An airplane is a flying machine.
Airplanes have wings.

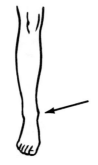

ankle   ankles

Your ankle is between your foot and
your leg.

apple   apples

An apple is a fruit that is good
to eat. Apples grow on trees.

apron   aprons

An apron covers your clothes. It
keeps them from getting dirty.

arm   arms

Your arm is between your shoulder
and your hand.

Things

arm   arms

Some chairs have arms. You can rest your arm on the arm of a chair.

back   backs

Your back is the part of your body opposite the front.

back   backs

A chair has a back. You can lean against the back of a chair when you sit down.

ball   balls

You can throw a ball or bounce it.

balloon   balloons

A balloon is a kind of rubber bag. You blow air into it.

Things

banana   bananas

A banana is a fruit that is good to eat. Bananas grow on trees.

bank   banks

A bank is a kind of box. You can put pennies in a bank to save them.

basket   baskets

A basket holds things. Some baskets are big. Some are little.

bat   bats

A bat is a long, thin piece of wood. You hit a ball with a bat.

bathing suit   bathing suits

A bathing suit is what you wear when you go swimming.

Things

bathtub   bathtubs

You fill a bathtub with water.
Then you sit in it to take a bath.

bean   beans

A bean is a kind of vegetable.
Beans are good to eat.

bed   beds

A bed is a soft place where you
can lie down. You sleep on a bed.

beet   beets

A beet is a kind of vegetable.
Some beets are red.

belt   belts

A belt is a strip of cloth or
leather. You wear a belt around
your waist.

Things

bicycle   bicycles

A bicycle has two wheels. You push pedals to make it go.

bike   bikes

Bike is another name for bicycle.

blanket   blankets

A blanket keeps you warm. Some blankets are soft and fluffy.

block   blocks

A block is a small piece of wood. Babies like to play with blocks.

blouse   blouses

A blouse is something a girl wears with a skirt.

Things

boat   boats

A boat is something to ride in on water. You cross a lake in a boat.

body   bodies

Every person has a body. Animals and fish have bodies, too.

bone   bones

There are many bones in your body. An animal has bones, too.

book   books

A book has sheets of paper inside two covers. Many books have colored pictures.

boot   boots

Boots keep your feet and legs dry. Wear boots when you go out in the snow or rain.

Things

box   boxes

A box holds things. There are all kinds of boxes. Some are little.

bracelet   bracelets

A bracelet is a chain that you wear around your arm.

bread

Bread is a kind of food. Bread with butter on it is good to eat.

brick   bricks

A brick is hard as a stone. Bricks are used to build houses and walls.

bridge   bridges

A bridge is a road or walk over water. You can cross a river by going over a bridge.

Things

broom   brooms

A broom is a brush with a long handle. You sweep with a broom.

brush   brushes

A brush is made of stiff hairs or wires. Some brushes are used to clean teeth or to paint houses.

building   buildings

A building has walls and a roof. Schools and houses are buildings.

bulletin board   bulletin boards

You can hang papers and pictures on a bulletin board.

bus   buses

A bus is like a large car. Some children ride in school buses.

Things

butter
You put butter on bread and toast.

button   buttons
A button is used to hold clothes together. A shirt has buttons down the front.

cake   cakes
Cake is something sweet to eat. Small cakes are cupcakes.

calendar   calendars
A calendar shows the months, weeks, and days of the year.

can   cans
A can is used to hold something. Many kinds of food are in cans.

Things

candle   candles

A candle gives light as it burns.
Birthday cakes often have candles.

candy   candies

Candy is good to eat. Some candy
is soft. Some is hard. Some
candies have nuts in them.

cap   caps

A cap is like a hat. You wear
a cap on your head.

capsule   capsules

The capsule is part of a spaceship.
Astronauts ride back to earth in
the capsule.

car   cars

A car is a machine that moves.
People ride in cars.

Things

carrot   carrots
A carrot is a vegetable. Carrots grow under the ground.

cereal   cereals
Cereal is a kind of food. Oatmeal and rice are cereals.

chain   chains
A chain is made of metal rings fastened together.

chair   chairs
You sit on a chair. A chair has a seat and a back.

chalk
Chalk is like a crayon. You write with chalk on a chalkboard.

chalkboard   chalkboards
A chalkboard is on the wall of the schoolroom.

Things

cherry   cherries

A cherry is a small, round fruit.
Cherries grow on trees.

chin   chins

Your chin is the part of your face
below your mouth.

clock   clocks

A clock shows what time it is.

clothes

People wear clothes. Dresses, pants,
sweaters, and shirts are clothes.
Hats and shoes are clothes, too.

cloud   clouds

A cloud often hides the sun in the
sky. Some clouds bring rain.

Things

coat   coats

A coat keeps you warm when it is cold outside.

comb   combs

Use a comb to keep your hair neat and in place.

cone   cones

A cone is like a cookie. It holds ice cream.

cookie   cookies

A cookie is a small, flat cake. Cookies taste good.

corn

Corn is a vegetable. Animals and people eat corn.

Things

crayon   crayons

Crayons are used for drawing and coloring pictures.

crib   cribs

A crib is a small bed. Mother puts the baby in his crib to sleep.

cup   cups

A cup is a dish to drink from. You drink cocoa from a cup.

cupcake   cupcakes

A cupcake is a small cake.

desk   desks

You write at a desk. Some desks have tops that roll down.

dish   dishes

A dish holds food. Cups and plates are dishes.

Things

doll   dolls

A doll is a toy person. Some children like to play with dolls.

door   doors

You open a door to go into a building or a room.

dress   dresses

A dress is something a girl wears. Dresses are clothes.

drum   drums

A drum makes a loud noise when you hit it.

dryer   dryers

You put clothes in the dryer after they are washed.

dustpan   dustpans

You sweep dust into a dustpan.

Things

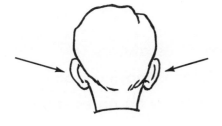

ear   ears
An ear is part of the body. You hear with your ears.

egg   eggs
An egg is good to eat. Some people have eggs for breakfast.

elbow   elbows
Your elbow is the middle part of your arm. You can bend your elbow.

elevator   elevators
An elevator is like a small room that moves. You ride up and down in an elevator.

eraser   erasers
An eraser rubs out what you have written. Erasers erase mistakes.

Things

escalator   escalators

An escalator is moving stairs.
You go upstairs on an escalator.

eye   eyes

Your eye is in your face. You see with your eyes.

face   faces

Your face is the front of your head. Everyone's face is different.

face   faces

The front of a clock is its face.

fan   fans

An electric fan helps keep you cool in hot weather.

Things

feather   feathers

A feather is part of a bird's body.
Feathers are soft and light.

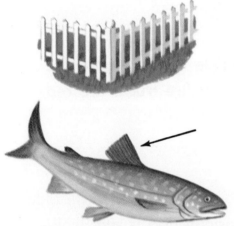

fence   fences

A fence around a garden or yard
keeps animals out.

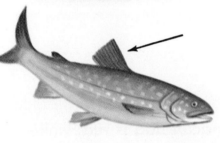

fin   fins

A fin is part of a fish's body.
A fish swims by moving its fins.

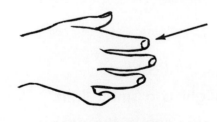

finger   fingers

A finger is part of your hand.

fire   fires

A fire is made by burning
something. Fires can be dangerous.

Things

fire hydrant   fire hydrants

Water comes from a fire hydrant.
Firemen put out fires with the water.

fire truck   fire trucks

Firemen ride to a fire on a fire
truck. Most fire trucks are red.

flag   flags

The American flag is red, white,
and blue.

flashlight   flashlights

A flashlight is a small light.
It helps you see in the dark.

flower   flowers

A flower grows from a seed or bulb.
Many flowers smell sweet.

Things

food   foods

Food is what you eat. Fruits, vegetables, and meats are food.

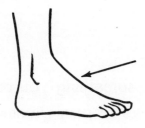

foot   feet

Your foot is at the end of your leg. People have two feet.

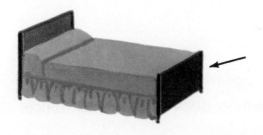

foot   feet

The foot of a bed is opposite the head of the bed.

fork   forks

You use a fork to lift food from a dish to your mouth.

fruit   fruits

Apples, oranges, and bananas are kinds of fruit.

Things

furniture

Chairs, tables, desks, and beds
are furniture.

game   games

A game is something you can play.
Children like to play games.

gate   gates

A gate is a door in a wall or fence.

glass   glasses

You can drink water or milk or
orange juice from a glass.

globe   globes

A globe is a round map of the world.
It looks like a ball.

Things

glove   gloves

You wear a glove on your hand.
Gloves keep your hands warm.

grass

Grass grows in fields, in parks, and
in yards.

greens

Greens are a vegetable. Greens
are good to eat.

guitar   guitars

You play a guitar with your fingers.

hair

Hair is what covers your head.
Some people have long hair.

Things

hamburger   hamburgers

Hamburger is a kind of meat. Most people like to eat a humburger in a bun.

hammer   hammers

You use a hammer to pound nails into wood.

hand   hands

Your hand is at the end of your arm.

hand   hands

The big hand and the little hand of a clock tell the time.

handkerchief   handkerchiefs

A handkerchief is a piece of cloth. You use your handkerchief when you blow your nose.

Things

hat   hats
You wear a hat on your head.

head   heads
Your head is part of your body. It is above your neck. Hair grows on your head.

head   heads
You put your head at the head of the bed when you lie down on it.

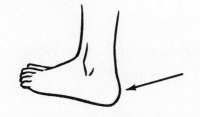

heel   heels
Your heel is the back part of your foot.

helicopter   helicopters
A helicopter is a flying machine. It has no wings.

Things

hoe   hoes

You use a hoe to break up dirt in a garden or yard.

honey

Honey is sweet. Honey tastes good on toast.

hood   hoods

A hood is something to wear on your head. Some jackets have hoods.

hook   hooks

A hook holds something. Hang your coat on a hook.

hot dog   hot dogs

A hot dog is a kind of meat. Some people put mustard on hot dogs.

Things

ice

Ice is frozen water. In winter there is ice on the pond.

ice cream

Ice cream is cold and sweet. It is good to eat with cake.

iron   irons

A hot iron makes clothes smooth.

ironing board   ironing boards

You put your clothes on an ironing board to iron them.

jacket   jackets

A jacket is a kind of short coat. Boys and girls both wear jackets.

Things

jacks

Jacks are little pieces of metal.
You play a game with them.

jar   jars

A jar holds things. Some jars are
made of glass.

jeans

Jeans are a kind of pants. Wear
jeans when you work outdoors.

jeep   jeeps

A jeep is a kind of car. Jeeps
can go across fields.

Jell-O

Jell-O is cool and sweet. It
tastes like some kind of fruit.

jelly   jellies

Jelly tastes good on toast or bread.

jump rope   jump ropes

You use a jump rope to play a game.
You swing the rope and jump over it.

114

Things

key   keys

A key locks and unlocks doors.
Put keys on a ring so you don't
lose them.

kite   kites

A kite will fly on a windy day.
Sometimes kites get caught in trees.

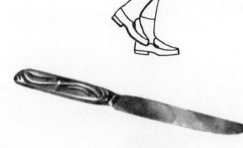

knee   knees

Your knee is part of your leg.
Your knees bend so you can walk.

knife   knives

A knife has a sharp edge. You cut
your food with a knife.

ladder   ladders

You climb up on a ladder to reach
high places.

Things

lamp   lamps

A lamp gives light. You turn on a lamp when it gets dark.

launching pad   launching pads

Rockets and spaceships are launched from a launching pad.

leaf   leaves

A leaf is part of a tree or plant. Most leaves are green.

leg   legs

Your leg is part of your body. You stand on your legs.

lemonade

Lemonade is a drink that is made from lemons and water and sugar.

Things

letter   letters

The first letter in a person's name is a capital.

lettuce

Lettuce is a vegetable. Lettuce is often used in a salad.

lightning

You see lightning in the sky when a storm is coming.

mailbox   mailboxes

You mail a letter when you put it in a mailbox.

map   maps

A map is a drawing. A map can help you find your way.

Things

meat   meats

Meat is a kind of food. Meat comes from animals.

merry-go-round   merry-go-rounds

Most people like to ride on a merry-go-round.

milk

Milk comes from cows. Drinking milk every day makes you grow.

mitten   mittens

A mitten has a thumb but no fingers. Mittens keep your hands warm when it is cold outside.

money

You buy things with money. People work to get money.

Things

moon

The moon is bright in the sky at night. A full moon is round.

mop   mops

You can use a mop to clean the floor. A mop has a long handle.

mouth   mouths

Your mouth is in your head. You eat and talk with your mouth.

movie   movies

A movie tells a story with pictures. Some movies are funny.

mustard

You can put mustard on a hot dog. Mustard is yellow.

Things

nail   nails

A nail holds pieces of wood together.
You pound nails with a hammer.

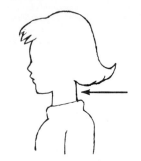

neck   necks

Your neck is the part of your body
between your head and shoulders.

nest   nests

A nest is the kind of home birds
build. Baby birds live in nests.

newspaper   newspapers

A newspaper tells what is happening.
People read newspapers every day.

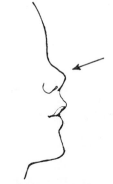

nose   noses

Your nose is part of your face.
You can smell things with your nose.

Things

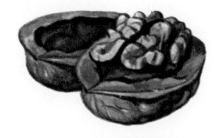

nut   nuts

A nut grows on a tree. Some nuts are good to eat.

orange   oranges

An orange is a fruit. Oranges grow on trees. Orange juice is good to drink.

pajamas

Pajamas are clothes some people wear to sleep in.

pan   pans

A pan is a dish you cook food in.

pants

Many people wear pants. Some pants are long. Some are short.

Things

paper   papers
You can write on paper. You can wrap something in paper, too.

parachute   parachutes
With a parachute, a person can jump from an airplane and come slowly to the ground.

paste
Paste makes pieces of paper stick together.

patch   patches
A patch is a piece of cloth. A patch will cover a hole in your dress or shirt.

pea   peas
A pea is a small green vegetable. Peas are good to eat.

Things

peanut butter

Peanut butter is good to eat on bread or crackers.

pear   pears

A pear is a fruit. Pears grow on trees.

pen   pens

You can write on paper with a pen. A pen has ink in it.

pencil   pencils

You write with a pencil. A pencil must have a sharp point.

piano   pianos

Some people can play music on a piano. Some people can't.

Things

pickle   pickles

A pickle tastes sour or sweet.
Most pickles are green.

picture   pictures

You can draw a picture or paint
a picture.

pie   pies

Pie is a good kind of food. Most
pies are sweet.

pillow   pillows

A pillow is soft. Put your head
on the pillow and go to sleep.

pitcher   pitchers

You can pour milk from a pitcher
into a glass.

Things

pizza   pizzas

Pizza is a kind of flat pie. It is very good to eat.

plane   planes

A plane is an airplane.

plant   plants

A plant grows in the ground. Trees are plants.

plate   plates

A plate is a flat dish.

popcorn

Popcorn is fun to pop and good to eat. Put salt and butter on it.

potato   potatoes

A potato is a vegetable. Sweet potatoes are yellow.

Things

pudding

Pudding is something soft to eat.

puppet   puppets

You put a puppet over your hand.
Your fingers make it move.

purse   purses

You carry things in a purse.

puzzle   puzzles

A puzzle is a kind of game. Some
puzzles are hard.

radio   radios

You can hear music on a radio.

rain

Rain is drops of water falling
from clouds.

Things

rainbow   rainbows

A rainbow has many colors. You see rainbows in the sky.

raincoat   raincoats

A raincoat helps keep you dry on a rainy day.

record player   record players

You play records on a record player. There are two record players in our school.

refrigerator   refrigerators

A refrigerator is cold inside. You keep food in it.

rice

Rice is a kind of cereal. Many people eat rice.

Things

rocket   rockets

A rocket blasts off from a launching pad. Some rockets go into space.

room   rooms

A room is part of a building. This room is a kitchen.

root   roots

A root is part of a plant. Roots grow under the ground.

rope   ropes

The boat was tied with rope. Some ropes are very thick.

salt

Many people put salt on food. Salt makes some food taste better.

Things

sand

Sand feels like sugar or salt.
Sand is not good to eat.

sandbox   sandboxes

A sandbox is a big box filled with sand. Children play in sandboxes.

sandwich   sandwiches

A sandwich is two pieces of bread with something in between them.

satellite   satellites

A satellite looks like a star. It moves in the sky.

saucer   saucers

A saucer is a small flat dish.
You set a cup on a saucer.

Things

saw   saws

You can cut wood with a saw.

scarf   scarves

You wear a scarf around your neck or on your head. Al has two scarves.

scissors

You can cut paper with scissors.

seed   seeds

If you plant a seed in the ground, it will grow.

seesaw   seesaws

It is fun to ride on a seesaw.

sewing machine   sewing machines

A person can make clothes with a sewing machine.

Things

shelf   shelves

There is a shelf for the dishes.
Are there any shelves for the
books and records?

shell   shells

A shell is a hard covering. Nuts
have shells.

ship   ships

A ship is a large boat. Ships
cross the ocean.

shirt   shirts

A boy or a girl may wear a shirt.
Some shirts have long sleeves.

shoe   shoes

A shoe is worn on a foot. Don't
wear shoes that are too short.

Things

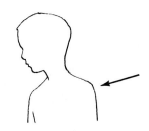

shoulder   shoulders

Your shoulder is between your neck and your arm.

shovel   shovels

You can pick up dirt or snow with a shovel. Power shovels are big digging machines.

sidewalk   sidewalks

Walk on the sidewalk. That's what sidewalks are for.

sink   sinks

You can wash dishes or get a drink of water at the sink.

skate   skates

A skate fits on your foot. You can go over ice with ice skates on. Roller skates have wheels.

Things

skirt   skirts

A skirt is something a girl can wear with a blouse or a shirt.

Skylab

Skylab is a space station that orbits the earth.

slacks

Slacks are a kind of pants. Both boys and girls wear slacks.

slide   slides

There is a slide on the playground. It is fun to go down a slide.

snow

Snow falls in tiny white flakes.

soap

Soap gets your hands clean.

sock   socks

A sock covers your foot. Be sure both socks are the same color.

Things

soup   soups

Soup is a kind of food. You eat soup with a spoon.

space suit   space suits

An astronaut wore a space suit on the moon.

spade   spades

A spade is a kind of shovel.

spoon   spoons

You eat ice cream and soup with a spoon. Some spoons are big.

stamp   stamps

A stamp is a piece of paper. You must put stamps on your letters.

star   stars

A star is far away. There are many stars in the sky at night.

Things

stem   stems

A stem is part of a plant. This rose has a long stem.

step   steps

A step is something you walk on to go up or down. Let's sit on the front steps for a while.

stick   sticks

A stick is a long, thin piece of wood. Throw a stick on the fire.

stone   stones

A stone is hard. Stones on the beach hurt your feet.

stool   stools

A stool is like a chair with no back or arms.

Things

stop sign   stop signs

A stop sign is red. Cars must stop at a stop sign.

stove   stoves

You can cook food on a stove.

street cleaner   street cleaners

A street cleaner is a big machine that cleans the streets.

sugar

Sugar is white. It tastes sweet.

suit   suits

A girl's suit may have a skirt and a jacket or pants and a jacket. A boy's suit has pants and a jacket.

sun

The sun makes the light every day.

sundae   sundaes

A chocolate sundae tastes good!

Things

sweater   sweaters

You can wear a sweater with pants or a skirt. Sweaters keep you warm.

swing   swings

A swing moves back and forth. There are swings on our playground.

table   tables

A table has legs and a flat top. You can put things on a table.

taco   tacos

A taco is a kind of food. You can buy tacos at a taco stand.

tail   tails

A tail is part of an animal's body.

taxicab   taxicabs

A taxicab is a car. You have to pay when you ride in it.

Things

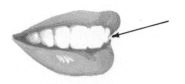

teeth

You bite and chew with your teeth.
Each one of your teeth is a tooth.

telephone   telephones

You can talk into a telephone and
hear someone answer.

television   TV

Do you like to watch television?
There is a good movie on TV today.

tent   tents

A tent is a house made of cloth.

thing   things

What one thing would you like to
have? Please put your things away.

thread

You sew clothes with thread.

Things

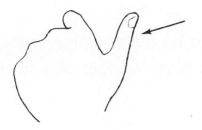

thumb   thumbs

Your thumb is the short, thick finger of your hand.

tie   ties

You wear a tie around your neck. Some ties are brightly colored.

tire   tires

A tire fits on the edge of a wheel. Tires are filled with air.

toast

Toast is bread that has been toasted until it is brown.

toaster   toasters

You put bread in a toaster to make toast.

Things

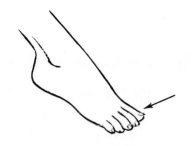

toe   toes

A toe is on the end of your foot.
People have five toes on each foot.

tooth   teeth

A tooth is one of your teeth.

toothbrush   toothbrushes

You brush your teeth with a
toothbrush.

top   tops

A top is a toy that spins. Some
tops make a noise.

tortilla   tortillas

A tortilla is a round, thin cake.

toy   toys

A toy is something to play with.
Dolls, balls, jacks, tops, and
kites are toys.

Things

tractor   tractors

A tractor is a kind of truck.
Farmers ride on tractors.

traffic light   traffic lights

A traffic light tells you when to
cross the street.

train   trains

A train has many cars hooked
together. Trains run on a track.

tree   trees

A tree has a trunk, branches, and
leaves. There are many different
kinds of trees.

tricycle   tricycles

A tricycle has three wheels.

Things

truck   trucks

A truck is a kind of car. Trucks carry heavy loads.

typewriter   typewriters

A typewriter is a machine for writing letters and numbers.

umbrella   umbrellas

An umbrella keeps the rain off your head.

vacuum cleaner   vacuum cleaners

A vacuum cleaner cleans rugs. It cleans floors and furniture, too.

vegetable   vegetables

A vegetable is a kind of food that grows as a plant. Peas and potatoes and beans are vegetables.

Things

vine   vines

A vine is a plant that grows along
the ground. Some vines grow up
on walls and fences.

wagon   wagons

You can put groceries in a wagon
and pull it home.

washer   washers

Throw all your dirty clothes in
the washer.

watch   watches

A watch is a clock you can wear
on your wrist.

water

You can drink water. You can
wash your face in water.

143

Things

wave   waves

A wave is like a hill of water.
There are big waves on the beach.

wheel   wheels

A wheel is round. Cars have four
wheels. Bicycles have two.

whistle   whistles

A whistle makes a loud noise if
you blow it.

window   windows

A window is an open place in a
wall. Houses have windows.

wing   wings

A wing is part of a bird. Birds
can't fly without wings.

Things

wrist   wrists

Your wrist is between your arm and your hand.

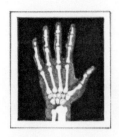

X ray   X rays

An X ray of your hand will show the bones.

yarn

Yarn is like thread. You make sweaters out of yarn.

yo-yo   yo-yos

A yo-yo is a toy. It moves up and down on a string.

zipper   zippers

A jacket may have a zipper instead of buttons.

Places

airport   airports

Airplanes land and take off from an airport.

apartment building apartment buildings

A big apartment building has many families living in it.

aquarium   aquariums

You can see many kinds of fish at an aquarium.

bakery   bakeries

Bread, cookies, pies, and cakes are made or sold at a bakery.

Places

beach   beaches

A beach is a strip of land next to the water. Some beaches are sandy.

bus station   bus stations

People wait for a bus at the bus station.

cafeteria   cafeterias

You eat at a cafeteria. You carry your food on a tray.

camp   camps

People who go to camp sometimes sleep in tents.

castle   castles

A castle has walls around it. In stories kings live in castles.

Places

center   centers

A neighborhood center is a good place to play games.

church   churches

Some people go to a church to worship and pray.

city   cities

Many people live in a city. Most cities have big buildings.

corner   corners

Two streets meet at a corner. Wait for your bus at the corner.

country

Country is the land outside a city. Farms are in the country.

Places

den   dens

A den is an animal's home. Bear cubs live in dens.

drugstore   drugstores

You buy medicine at a drugstore.

dump   dumps

A dump is a place to throw things you don't want any longer.

earth

The earth is a huge planet. It has mountains and oceans and rivers. All the people and animals live on the earth.

factory   factories

People make things at a factory. TV sets are made in factories.

Places

fairground   fairgrounds

You go to the fairground to see the fair.

farm   farms

A farmer raises animals and food on a farm.

field   fields

A field is part of a farm. Corn grows in fields.

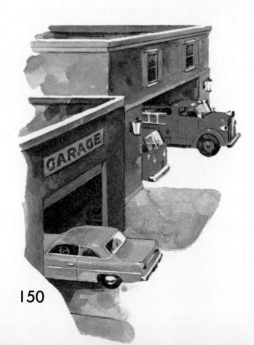

firehouse   firehouses

Fire trucks are kept in a firehouse.

garage   garages

Cars are kept or fixed at a garage. Mechanics fix cars in garages.

Places

garden   gardens

You can grow vegetables and flowers in a garden.

gas station   gas stations

Drivers buy gas at a gas station.

harbor   harbors

A harbor is a safe place for boats to stay.

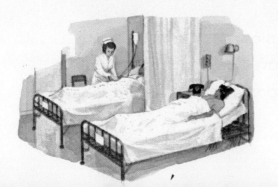

hospital   hospitals

A hospital is a good place for sick people. They are cared for at a hospital.

Places

hotel hotels

A hotel has rooms for people to sleep in. People pay to stay overnight in a hotel.

house houses

A house is a building for people to live in.

library libraries

Books are kept in a library. You can borrow books at most libraries.

moon

The moon is a satellite. It moves around the earth. Astronauts have been to the moon.

Places

mosque   mosques

Some people go to a mosque to
worship and pray.

motel   motels

People can stay overnight at a
motel when they take a long trip.

mountain   mountains

A mountain is a very high hill.
Some mountains have snow on top
even in summer.

museum   museums

You can see dinosaur bones at a
museum. You can see stuffed
animals and stuffed birds, too.

Places

neighborhood   neighborhoods

A neighborhood is the part of town where you live. There is a drugstore in our neighborhood.

observatory   observatories

At an observatory scientists watch the stars move.

office   offices

People work in an office.

palace   palaces

A king or queen lives in a palace. Palaces are huge houses with beautiful gardens and trees.

154

Places

park   parks

A park has grass and trees. Let's have a picnic in the park.

parking lot   parking lots

A parking lot is a place to park many cars.

place   places

What is the most interesting place you have ever seen? There are many places to see in the city.

playground   playgrounds

You go to the playground to play. Some playgrounds have swings and slides and merry-go-rounds.

Places

post office   post offices

You can mail a letter at a post office. Mail carriers bring mail to you from the post office.

ranch   ranches

A ranch is a kind of farm where cattle or sheep are raised.

restaurant   restaurants

It is fun to eat at a restaurant. You pay for the food. You eat anything you want.

Places

school   schools

Children go to school to learn.

shop   shops

A shop is a kind of store. You buy gifts at a gift shop.

shopping center   shopping centers

There are many stores in a big shopping center.

skating rink   skating rinks

You see some good skaters at a skating rink.

Places

sky   skies

The sky is the air above us. Some skies look very blue.

space   spaces

There is space between the earth and the moon. Astronauts go into space to get to the moon.

store   stores

You buy things in a store. There are many kinds of stores.

street   streets

Our town has one main street. Big cities have many streets. What street does he live on?

Places

supermarket   supermarkets
A supermarket is a large store.
You choose what you want to buy.

swimming pool   swimming pools
A swimming pool is a place to
swim. Some swimming pools are
outdoors. Some are indoors.

synagogue   synagogues
Some people go to a synagogue
to worship and pray.

Places

theater   theaters

You can see a movie or a play at a theater. Our town has a theater and a drive-in movie.

town   towns

A town is a small city.

valley   valleys

The place between two mountains or hills is called a valley.

village   villages

A village is a small town. There are only a few houses in a village.

Places

woods

Trees grow close together in the woods. You can get lost there.

world

The world is the earth and everything on it.

yard   yards

A yard is the land and space around a house. Many people plant flowers and grass in their yards.

zoo   zoos

Wild animals are kept at a zoo. You go to the zoo to see them.

Words That Help

Some words tell what kind.

Some words tell what color.

Some words help tell how much or how many.

Some words tell how.

Some words help tell when.

Some words help tell where.

Some words tell which one.

Some words tell what kind.

Jerry has a big dog.

We all chose chocolate ice cream.

Mom is proud of her clean car.

Wear a lot of clothes on a cold day.

Some words tell what kind.

It's spooky on a dark night.

An electric fan helps keep you cool.

A fat puppy can't run very fast.

He's a very friendly dog.

Some words tell what kind.

The funny clown made us laugh.

A hot iron can burn your shirt.

A little kangaroo is easy to carry.

This sweater has long sleeves.

Some words tell what kind.

We have new kittens at home.

Mother said it was a noisy party.

The old man was sitting in the sun.

Wear your boots on a rainy day.

166

Some words tell what kind.

We saw a sad movie on TV.

A tall person can see a lot.

The circus had wild animals.

It's hard to walk on a windy day.

Some words tell what color.

black

blue

brown

gray

green

lavender

orange

pink

purple

red

white

yellow

Some words help tell how much or how many.

a few peanuts

lots of peanuts

a little ice cream   a lot of ice cream

All the children are smiling.

None of the children are smiling.

Some words help tell how much or how many.

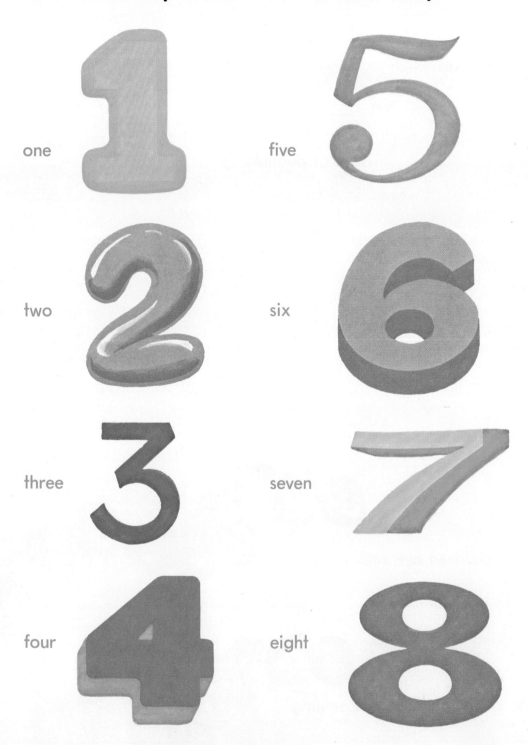

one

two

three

four

five

six

seven

eight

170

Some words help tell how much or how many.

nine
9

penny
cent

ten
10

nickel

dime

eleven
11

quarter

dollar

twelve
12

Some words tell how.

He skates badly.

The sun shone brightly.

He wrote his name carefully.

She wrote her name carelessly.

Racing cars go fast.

Some words tell how.

He hit the ball hard.

She sadly waved good-by.

He ate his ice-cream cone slowly.

The horse stopped suddenly.

They do their work well.

Some words help tell when.

before

after

early

late

always

never

Some words help tell when.

yesterday

today

tomorrow

Some words help tell when.

	Picnic → Bill
Sunday	Piano lesson → (Mother)
Monday	Basketball Game (with brother, Jim)
Tuesday	Aunt Sue coming to dinner (Mother)
Wednesday	Take milk money (B.)
Thursday	Stay up late, watch TV ok by Dad
Friday	
Saturday	Go to Grandma's Bill

Some words help tell when.

January

February

March

April

May

June

July

August

September

October

November

December

spring

summer

fall
autumn

winter

Some words help tell where.

The flag is above the school.

The playground is by the school.

A slide is across from the swings.

A boy is ahead of the girl.

A fence is around the playground.

Some words help tell where.

A boy is at the chalkboard.

The teacher is behind her desk.

A bookcase is below the windows.

A girl is beside the bookcase.

179

Some words help tell where.

A lamp is between the chairs.

Mother is down at the door.

Billy is taking a book from
the shelf.

Two goldfish are in the bowl.

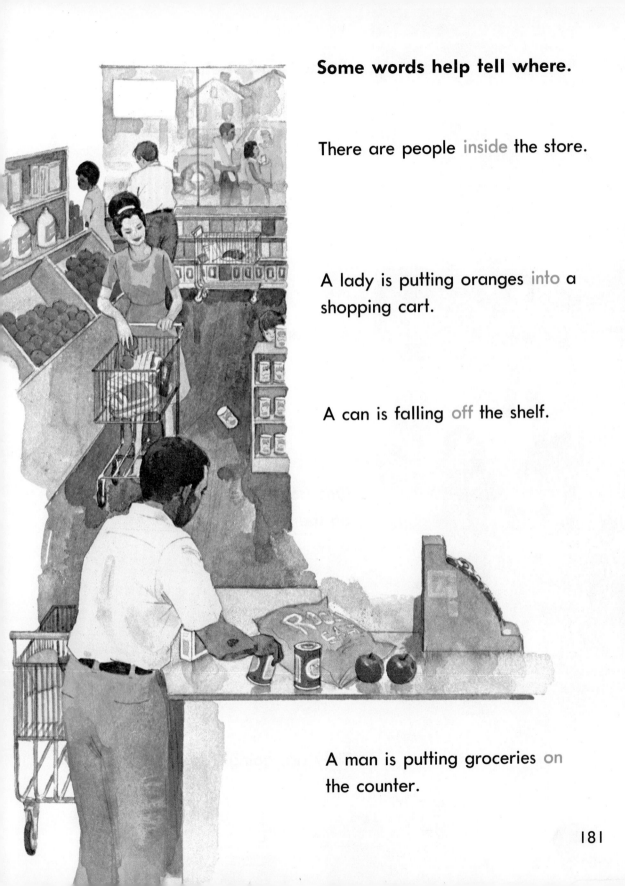

Some words help tell where.

There are people inside the store.

A lady is putting oranges into a shopping cart.

A can is falling off the shelf.

A man is putting groceries on the counter.

Some words help tell where.

The boy is running out the door.

His friends are outside the house.

One boy is jumping over a puddle on the sidewalk.

They are going to the park.

Some words help tell where.

The bench is under a tree.

A squirrel is underneath the bench.

A bird is up in the tree.

A butterfly is sitting upon a leaf.

183

Some words tell which one.

Ann took the first seat in the row.

Danny took the last seat in the row.

The pencil is in Lucy's left hand.

Eric is standing on his right foot.

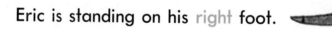

That book is the one I want.

Would this book do?

INDEX

My First Picture Dictionary, which presents 865 words, is the second in a set of three reference books. Together with the other two—My Pictionary, for use in kindergarten, and My Second Picture Dictionary, to be used in second grade—this book may be used with the Scott Foresman Reading Systems, the Coordinated Communications Program, Open Highways, or any other primary program. These reference books, along with the exercise books for the first and second picture dictionaries, begin the sequential K–12 pictionary/dictionary program of Scott, Foresman and Company.

In My Pictionary words are presented as labeled pictures grouped in nine color-coded categories. In this book the same words—plus 330 additional ones—are arranged alphabetically within the familiar categories. Here different forms of these words are used in easy-to-understand sentences.

a

above	178
across	178
after	174
ahead	178
airplane	88
airport	146
all	169
alligator	26
always	174
animal	26
ankle	88
answer	50
ant	26
apartment building	146
apple	88
April	177
apron	88
aquarium	146
arm	88, 89
around	178
artist	6

astronaut	6
at	179
August	177
aunt	6
autumn	177

b

baby	6
back	89
badly	172
bake	50
baker	7
bakery	146
ball	89
balloon	89
banana	90
bank	90
barber	7
basket	90
bat	26, 50, 90
bathing suit	90
bathtub	91
beach	147

bean	91
bear	26
beaver	27
bed	91
bee	27
beet	91
beetle	27
before	174
begin	50
behind	179
below	179
belt	91
bend	51
beside	179
between	180
bicycle	92
big	163
bike	92
bird	27
bite	51
black	168
blanket	92
block	92
blouse	92
blow	51

blue 168
blue jay 27
boat 93
body 93
bone 93
book 93
boot 93
bounce 51
box 94
boy 7
bracelet 94
bread 94
break 52
brick 94
bride 7
bridegroom 7
bridge 94
brightly 172
broom 95
brother 8
brown 168
brownie 46
brush 52, 95
bug 28
build 52
building 95
bulletin board 95
bus 95
bus driver 11
bus station 147
butter 96
butterfly 28
button 52, 96
buy 53
by 178

c

cafeteria 147
cake 96
calendar 96
calf 28

camel 28
camp 147
can 96
canary 28
candle 97
candy 97
cap 97
capsule 97
car 97
cardinal 29
carefully 172
carelessly 172
carpenter 8
carrot 98
carry 53
castle 147
cat 29
catch 53
caterpillar 29
cent 171
center 148
centipede 29
cereal 98
chain 98
chair 98
chalk 98
chalkboard 98
checker 8
cherry 99
chicken 29
child 8
chin 53, 99
chipmunk 29
chocolate 163
choose 54
chop 54
church 148
city 148
clap 54
clean 163
clerk 9
climb 54
clock 99

clothes 99
cloud 99
clown 9
coat 100
cold 163
color 55, 168
colt 30
comb 55, 100
come 55
cone 100
cook 9
cookie 100
corn 100
corner 148
country 148
cousin 9
cow 30
cowboy 9
crawl 55
crayon 101
crib 101
crow 30
cry 56
cub 30
cup 101
cupcake 101
custodian 10
cut 56

d

dad 10
dance 56
dark 164
daughter 10
December 177
deer 30
den 149
dentist 10
desk 101
dial 56
dig 57

dime 171
dinosaur 31
dish 101
dive 57
diver 11
do 57
doctor 11
dog 31
doll 102
dollar 171
dolphin 31
donkey 31
door 102
down 180
dragon 46
draw 57
dress 58, 102
drink 58
drive 58
driver 11
drop 58
druggist 11
drugstore 149
drum 102
dryer 102
duck 31
dump 59, 149
dustpan 102
dwarf 46

e

eagle 32
ear 103
early 174
earth 149
eat 59
egg 103
eight 170
elbow 103
electric 164
electrician 11

elephant 32
elevator 103
eleven 171
elf 46
erase 59
eraser 103
escalator 104
eye 104

f

face 104
factory 149
fairground 150
fairy 46
fall 59, 177
family 12-13
fan 104
farm 150
farmer 14
fast 172
fat 164
father 14
feather 105
February 177
feed 60
feet 107
fence 105
few 169
field 150
fight 60
fin 105
find 60
finger 105
fire 105
firefighter 14
firehouse 150
fire hydrant 106
fireman 14
fire truck 106
first 184
fish 32, 60

five 170
fix 61
flag 106
flashlight 106
flower 106
fly 32, 61
fold 61
follow 61
food 107
foot 107
forget 62
fork 107
four 170
fox 33
freeze 62
Friday 176
friendly 164
frog 33
from 180
frown 62
fruit 107
funny 165
furniture 108

g

game 108
garage 150
garden 151
gas station 151
gate 108
geese 34
gerbil 33
ghost 47
giant 47
giraffe 33
girl 14
give 62
glass 108
globe 108
glove 109
go 63

goat 33
goblin 47
goldfish 34
goose 34
grandchild 15
granddaughter 15
grandfather 15
grandmother 15
grandson 16
grass 109
gray 168
green 168
greens 109
grow 63
guard 16
guitar 109
guppy 34
gymnast 16

h

hair 109
hamburger 110
hammer 63, 110
hamster 34
hand 110
handkerchief 110
hang 63
harbor 151
hard 173
hat 111
head 111
heel 111
helicopter 111
help 64
hen 34
hide 64
hippopotamus 35
hit 64
hoe 112
honey 112
hood 112

hook 112
hop 64
horse 35
hospital 151
hot 165
hot dog 112
hotel 152
house 152
hug 65
hummingbird 35

i

ice 113
ice cream 113
in 180
insect 35
inside 181
into 181
iron 65, 113
ironing board 113

j

jacket 113
Jack Frost 47
jacks 114
janitor 16
January 177
jar 114
jeans 114
jeep 114
Jell-O 114
jelly 114
judge 16
July 177
jump 65
jump rope 114
June 177

k

kangaroo 35
key 115
kick 65
kid 36
king 47
kite 115
kitten 36
knee 115
knife 115
knight 48
know 66
koala 36

l

ladder 115
ladybug 36
lamb 36
lamp 116
last 184
late 174
laugh 66
launching pad 116
lavender 168
leaf 116
left 184
leg 116
lemonade 116
leopard 36
letter 117
lettuce 117
librarian 17
library 152
lie 66
lifeguard 17
lightning 117
lion 37

little 165, 169
lizard 37
long 165
lot 169
lots 169

m

magician 17
mailbox 117
mail carrier 17
mailman 17
make 66
mama 18
man 18
map 117
March 177
May 177
meat 118
mechanic 18
men 18
merry-go-round 118
mice 37
milk 67, 118
miner 18
mitten 118
mix 67
mom 18
Monday 176
money 118
monkey 37
moon 119, 152
mop 67, 119
mosque 153
mosquito 37
motel 153
mother 19
mountain 153
mouse 37
mouth 119
move 67
movie 119

museum 153
mustard 119

n

nail 120
neck 120
neighbor 19
neighborhood 154
nephew 19
nest 120
never 174
new 166
newspaper 120
nickel 171
niece 19
night watchman 25
nine 171
noisy 166
none 169
nose 120
November 177
nurse 20
nut 121

o

observatory 154
October 177
off 181
office 154
ogre 48
oil 68
old 166
on 181
one 170
open 68
operator 20
opossum 38
orange 121, 168
orange juice 121
orbit 68
out 182

outside 182
over 182
owl 38

p

paint 68
painter 20
pajamas 121
palace 154
pan 121
panda 38
pants 121
papa 20
paper 122
parachute 122
parakeet 38
parent 20
park 155
parking lot 155
parrot 38
paste 69, 122
patch 69, 122
pea 122
peacock 39
peanut butter 123
pear 123
peel 69
pen 123
pencil 123
penguin 39
penny 171
people 21
person 21
photographer 21
piano 123
pickle 124
picture 124
pie 124
pig 39
pigeon 39
Pilgrim 21

pillow 124
pilot 22
pink 168
pirate 48
pitcher 124
pizza 125
place 155
plane 125
plant 69, 125
plate 125
play 70
playground 155
plumber 22
point 70
policeman 22
police officer 22
policewoman 22
pony 40
popcorn 125
porcupine 40
postman 22
post office 156
potato 125
pour 70
power shovel 132
prince 48
princess 48
principal 22
print 70
pudding 125
pull 71
puppet 126
puppy 40
purple 168
purse 126
push 71
puzzle 126

q

quarter 171
queen 49

r

rabbit 40
raccoon 40
radio 126
rain 71, 126
rainbow 127
raincoat 127
rainy 166
rake 71
ranch 156
rat 41
record player 127
red 168
refrigerator 127
reindeer 41
relative 23
reporter 23
restaurant 156
rhinoceros 41
rice 127
ride 72
right 184
rise 72
robin 41
rock 72
rocket 128
roll 72
room 128
rooster 41
root 128
rope 73, 128
run 73

s

sad 167
sadly 173
salesperson 23
salt 128

sand 129
sandbox 129
sandwich 129
satellite 129
Saturday 176
saucer 129
saw 73, 130
say 73
scare 74
scarf 130
school 157
scissors 130
seal 42
see 74
seed 130
seesaw 130
September 177
seven 170
sew 74
sewing machine 130
shake 74
sheep 42
shelf 131
shell 131
ship 131
shirt 131
shoe 131
shop 157
shopping center 157
shoulder 132
shovel 75, 132
show 75
shrink 75
shut 75
sidewalk 132
sing 76
sink 76, 132
sister 23
six 170
skate 76, 132
skating rink 157
skirt 133
skunk 42

sky 158
Skylab 133
slacks 133
sleep 76
slide 77, 133
slowly 173
smile 77
snail 42
snake 42
snow 77, 133
soap 133
sock 133
son 23
soup 134
space 158
space suit 134
spade 77, 134
sparrow 43
speak 78
spider 43
spill 78
splash 78
spoon 134
spread 78
spring 177
squeeze 79
squirrel 43
stamp 134
stand 79
star 134
starfish 43
stem 135
step 79, 135
stick 79, 135
stir 80
stone 135
stool 135
stop 80
stop sign 136
store 158
stove 136
street 158
street cleaner 136

suddenly 173
sugar 136
suit 136
summer 177
sun 136
sundae 136
Sunday 176
superintendent 24
supermarket 159
swan 43
sweater 137
sweep 80
swim 80
swimming pool 159
swing 81, 137
synagogue 159

t

table 137
taco 137
tail 137
take 81
talk 81
tall 167
taxicab 137
teacher 24
tear 81
teeth 138
telephone 138
television 138
tell 82
ten 171
tent 138
that 184
theater 160
thing 138
this 184
thread 138
three 170
throw 82
thumb 139

Thursday 176
tie 82, 139
tiger 44
tire 139
to 182
toad 44
toast 82, 139
toaster 139
today 175
toe 140
tomorrow 175
tooth 140
toothbrush 140
top 140
tortilla 140
touch 83
town 160
toy 140
tractor 141
traffic light 141
train 141
tree 141
tricycle 141
trim 83
troll 49
truck 142
truck driver 11
Tuesday 176
turkey 44
turn 83
turtle 44
TV 138
twelve 171
twin 24
two 170
typewriter 142
typist 24

u

umbrella 142
uncle 25

191

under 183
underneath 183
unicorn 49
up 183
upon 183

v

vacuum cleaner 142
valley 160
vegetable 142
village 160
vine 143

w

wade 83
wagon 143
waiter 25
waitress 25
walk 84
wash 84
washer 143
watch 84, 143
watchman 25

water 84, 143
wave 144
wear 85
weave 85
Wednesday 176
weigh 85
well 173
whale 44
wheel 144
whistle 85, 144
white 168
wild 167
wind 86
window 144
windy 167
wing 144
wink 86
winter 177
witch 49
wizard 49
wolf 45
woman 25
woodpecker 45
woods 161
work 86
world 161
worm 45

wrap 86
wrist 145
write 87

x

X ray 145

y

yard 161
yarn 145
yawn 87
yell 87
yellow 168
yesterday 175
yo-yo 145

z

zebra 45
zip 87
zipper 145
zoo 161